Vegetation Community Monitoring at Fort Frederica National Monument, 2009

Natural Resource Data Series NPS/SECN/NRDS—2012/251

Michael W. Byrne and Sarah L. Corbett

USDI National Park Service
Southeast Coast Inventory and Monitoring Network
Cumberland Island National Seashore
101 Wheeler Street
Saint Marys, Georgia, 31558

and

Joseph C. DeVivo

USDI National Park Service
Southeast Coast Inventory and Monitoring Network
University of Georgia
160 Phoenix Road, Phillips Lab
Athens, Georgia, 30605

February 2012

U.S. Department of the Interior
National Park Service
Natural Resource Stewardship and Science
Fort Collins, Colorado

The National Park Service, Natural Resource Stewardship and Science office in Fort Collins, Colorado publishes a range of reports that address natural resource topics of interest and applicability to a broad audience in the National Park Service and others in natural resource management, including scientists, conservation and environmental constituencies, and the public.

The Natural Resource Data Series is intended for the timely release of basic data sets and data summaries. Care has been taken to assure accuracy of raw data values, but a thorough analysis and interpretation of the data has not been completed. Consequently, the initial analyses of data in this report are provisional and subject to change.

All manuscripts in the series receive the appropriate level of peer review to ensure that the information is scientifically credible, technically accurate, appropriately written for the intended audience, and designed and published in a professional manner.

This report received informal peer review by subject-matter experts who were not directly involved in the collection, analysis, or reporting of the data.

Data in this report were collected and analyzed using methods based on established, peer-reviewed protocols and were analyzed and interpreted within the guidelines of the protocols.

Views, statements, findings, conclusions, recommendations, and data in this report do not necessarily reflect views and policies of the National Park Service, U.S. Department of the Interior. Mention of trade names or commercial products does not constitute endorsement or recommendation for use by the U.S. Government.

This report is available from (http://science.nature.nps.gov/im/units/secn) and the Natural Resource Publications Management website (http://www.nature.nps.gov/publications/nrpm/).

Please cite this publication as:

NPS 369/112890, February 2012

Contents

Figures

Tables

List of Terms

Absolute cover: The total amount of ground surface that is covered by each species or group. Describes the amount of cover that each species or group represents in a stratum. Expressed as a percentage. Can exceed 100% due to overlap. The total cover of each species or group divided by the total possible cover for a plot.

Canopy species: Woody species known to occur in the midstory or overstory of the canopy, or shrub species that grow greater than or equal to 4 cm DBH and measureable at breast height (1.4 m).

Canopy stratum: The structural zone above 1.1 m (i.e., elbow height of a typical observer as per densiometer instructions) and consists of all live and dead plant material that affects the amount of light penetrating to the ground. This includes individual elements whose cover is also potentially measured and accounted for in the shrub- or groundcover-stratum measurements, but exceeds 1.1 m in height, is detected by the densiometer, and contributes to canopy cover. Also referred to as the midstory, overstory, or sub-canopy.

Cover: The vertical projection of the outermost extent of a species, or the extent of the shadow cast by the species if the sun were directly overhead. Foliar cover.

DBH: Diameter at breast height, or 1.4 m above the ground's surface.

Frequency: The number of times a species or group is detected in a plot, expressed as a percentage. Provides information on regularity at which a species or group is encountered.

Groundcover stratum: The structural zone that consists of all non-woody species (i.e., forbs and graminoids), and all woody species (i.e., shrubs and trees) with a DBH of less than 1 cm and seedlings 30 cm or less in height.

Relative cover: The cover of each species or group as a function of all other plant species that occurred in a plot. Describes the percentage of cover that each species represents out of the total vegetative cover in a stratum. Expressed as a percentage. Always sums to 100%. The total cover of each species or group divided by the sum of the cover of all other species that occur in a plot.

Seedlings: Woody dicotyledonous plants less than 30 cm in height.

Shrub stratum: All woody species greater than 30 cm in height with a DBH of 1–4 cm.

Stratum: A structural size category of vegetation at a site. These are the canopy, shrub, and groundcover layers.

Executive Summary

In 2009, the National Park Service (NPS) Southeast Coast Network (SECN) Inventory and Monitoring Network began collecting vegetation community data as part the NPS Vital Signs monitoring program. Information collected under this Vital Sign will be used to help managers make better-informed decisions by understanding trends and variability related to plant species, frequency of occurrence, percent cover, diversity, and distribution in the groundcover, shrub, and canopy strata.

Within each stratum, vegetation communities were sampled using a hybrid of methods used by the North Carolina Vegetation Survey nested-subplot design (Peet et al. 1998) within a circular plot similar to the Forest Inventory and Analysis protocol (Bechtold and Patterson 2005). This report summarizes vegetation community data collected at Fort Frederica National Monument in 2009.

1. Data were collected at eight spatially-balanced random locations at the Monument. The findings below apply only to portions of the park that meet the following site selection criteria:

   a) Sites are located within park boundaries and ownership.

   b) Sites must be sampleable within safety guidelines.

   c) Sites cannot be located in wholly non-natural areas, open water, or areas where application of the methods is inappropriate (such as marshes).

2. Sampling activities occurred at the Monument from 7/20 to 7/24/2009.

3. Monitoring efforts resulted in the addition of 20 species, subspecies, or varieties to the park's species list.

4. Absolute canopy cover across the park was approximately 77%.

5. Virginia live oak (*Quercus virginiana*) had the largest average diameter at breast height of any canopy species at the park.

6. One live redbay (*Persea borbonia*) of canopy size was detected.

7. Two redbay seedlings were detected.

8. Non-native species of potential management concern were detected in the canopy and shrub strata [including Chinese privet (*Ligustrum sinense*) and camphortree (*Cinnamomum camphora*)].

9. Yaupon holly (*Ilex vomitoria*), wax myrtle (*Morella cerifera*), and laurel oak (*Quercus laurifolia*) were the most frequently occurring species in the shrub stratum.

10. Wax myrtle had the highest relative cover in the shrub stratum. Yaupon holly had the highest absolute cover in the shrub stratum.

11. Yaupon holly and wax myrtle were the most frequently occurring species in the groundcover stratum.

12. Yaupon holly had the highest relative cover in the groundcover stratum. Bahiagrass (*Paspalum notatum*) had the highest absolute cover in the groundcover stratum.

13. The full dataset, and associated metadata, can be acquired from the data store at http://science.nature.nps.gov/nrdata/

Introduction

Overview

Vegetation communities provide many ecosystem services. Among their many functions, they are an important component of food webs and wildlife habitat for many species, and serve as a carbon sink, produce oxygen, cycle nutrients and energy through an ecosystem, influence the local climate, improve water quality, and moderate flooding and erosion. Plant communities also respond to multiple stressors such as changes in air quality, hydrology, disturbance regimes, and climate. Determining trends in vegetation communities is vital to understanding the ecological processes occurring at a site, and identifying stressors and their impacts.

Vegetation communities are dynamic entities with constant changes in composition, cover, distribution, and structure that reflect stressor response, natural or anthropogenic in origin. Disturbance is the primary stressor and regulating mechanism of SECN vegetation communities. The timing, type, and extent of the disturbance generally evokes a distinguishable response in the species composition, diversity, and structure of the landscape (Foster et al. 1998, Turner et al. 1990). The primary natural-disturbance processes in SECN parks are fire and weather (e.g., hurricanes, drought). Anthropogenic influences include fire suppression, landscape fragmentation, altered hydrology, and non-native species introduction.

The SECN is composed of a diverse assemblage of vegetation communities. Approximately 180 vegetation associations (i.e., fine-resolution floristic description), as defined by the National Vegetation and Classification System (FGDC 2008), occur in the SECN. These communities vary widely in distribution, species composition, and structure, and include sparsely vegetated primary dune communities, late successional old-growth bottomland hardwood forest communities, and highly diverse herbaceous-dominated mesic pine savannah communities.

Given the widespread anthropogenic influences in SECN parks and the importance of vegetation communities, quantifying trends in plant cover, frequency, diversity, and distribution is a high priority (DeVivo et al. 2008). Evaluating trends in these metrics provides measures for assessing the ecological integrity and sustainability of southeastern ecosystems, and identifying the need for specific management activities on our park lands. The National Park Service Omnibus Management Act of 1998, and other reinforcing policies and regulations, require park managers "to establish baseline information and to provide information on the long-term trends in the condition of National Park System resources" (Title II, Sec. 204). The vegetation-community monitoring data summarized herein is a tool to assist park managers in fulfilling this mandate.

This report summarizes data collected as a part of the SECN's Vegetation Community Vital Signs monitoring efforts.

Monitoring Objective

- Determine trends in plant species frequency, percent cover, diversity, and distribution in the groundcover, shrub, and canopy strata.

Methods

Study Area

Fort Frederica National Monument (FOFR) is on St. Simons Island in southeast Georgia (Figure 1). The monument is divided by the Frederica River, one of the primary salt marsh rivers in the Brunswick area, with 40 ha (99 ac) of marsh lands at the Frederica site on the west side of the river and approximately 55 ha (137 ac) of uplands adjoining the east side of the river. The focal area of the park is the Revolutionary-era townsite of Fort Frederica, and this area is maintained as a mowed field. The separate Bloody Marsh site is approximately 3 ha (8 ac), half of which are tidal marsh. The salt marsh is dominated by cordgrass (*Spartina* spp.), and the uplands are a mix of coastal maritime hammock dominated by Virginia live oak (*Quercus virginiana*) and a small component of slash pine (*Pinus elliottii*).

Fort Frederica was an important colonial settlement site. Later, during the Revolutionary War, Bloody Marsh was a significant battle site. The site of Fort Frederica has undergone several human-induced changes over the past 200 years that have altered the area from its pre-colonial climax maritime live oak hammock condition (Bratton 1983). These include the original occupation of the site as a fort, farming of for corn, tobacco, and cotton, and later as a pine plantation. Some drainage ditches were installed for agricultural purposes and still exist in the Monument. Prolonged drainage of these areas has facilitated a shift in the vegetation composition from wetland to upland species (Bratton 1983).

Figure 1. Location of Fort Frederica National Monument.

FOFR has 282 known vascular-plant species, subspecies, and varieties (NPSpecies 2011), including 20 species, subspecies, and varieties added to the species based on these monitoring efforts (Appendix A, Table 2). Species that occur in the Monument with potential to cause management problems include Japanese and Chinese privet (*Ligustrum japonicum* and *L. sinense*), Chinese wisteria (*Wisteria sinensis*), tallowtree (*Sapium sebiferum*), largeleaf lantana (*Lantana camara*), and camphortree (*Cinnamomum camphora*).

Redbay (*Persea borbonia*) is a critical native element of the coastal maritime hammock community and also serves as an important habitat component for many vertebrates, invertebrates, vascular plants, and non-vascular plants. Occurrences of native redbay throughout coastal southeastern U.S. are in rapid decline due to the introduction of a fungal pathogen, laurel wilt (*Raffaelea lauricola*), whose vector is the non-native redbay ambrosia beetle (from Asia) (*Xyleborus glabratus*). The non-native redbay ambrosia beetle, and laurel wilt, does occur at FOFR. Since the beetle's initial detection in 2002 (Haack 2006, Rabaglia 2003), and the subsequent lethality of laurel wilt to redbay, this pathogen has had a profound adverse effect on redbay across the Monument and in over 60 counties in the southeastern U.S. (Fraedrich et al. 2008), primarily along the Atlantic coast (http://www.fs.fed.us/r8/foresthealth/laurelwilt/dist_map.shtml). Extensive multi-agency efforts are currently underway to further understand this pathogen, identify possible methods of eradication, and identify mitigation procedures to ensure the persistence of redbay and other potentially susceptible members of the Lauraceae. The breadth of the adverse ecological impacts of the loss of redbay in the coastal maritime hammock is unknown.

Sampling Design

To allow for park-wide inference, the park's administrative boundary was used as the sampling frame, which was divided into a systematic 0.5-ha grid; the center point of each grid cell served as the potential sampling site and the grid cell served as the macroplot. A spatially-balanced sample was drawn from this grid using the Reversed Randomized Quadrant-Recursive Raster (RRQRR) algorithm (Theobald et al. 2007). Alternate points were used when selection criteria (i.e., including safety and access issues) were not met. A sample size of eight was chosen after consideration of park size, hypothesized variability, and logistical issues regarding travel time and conducting monitoring activities in five to six park units per year. The park was sampled from 7/20 to 7/24/2009.

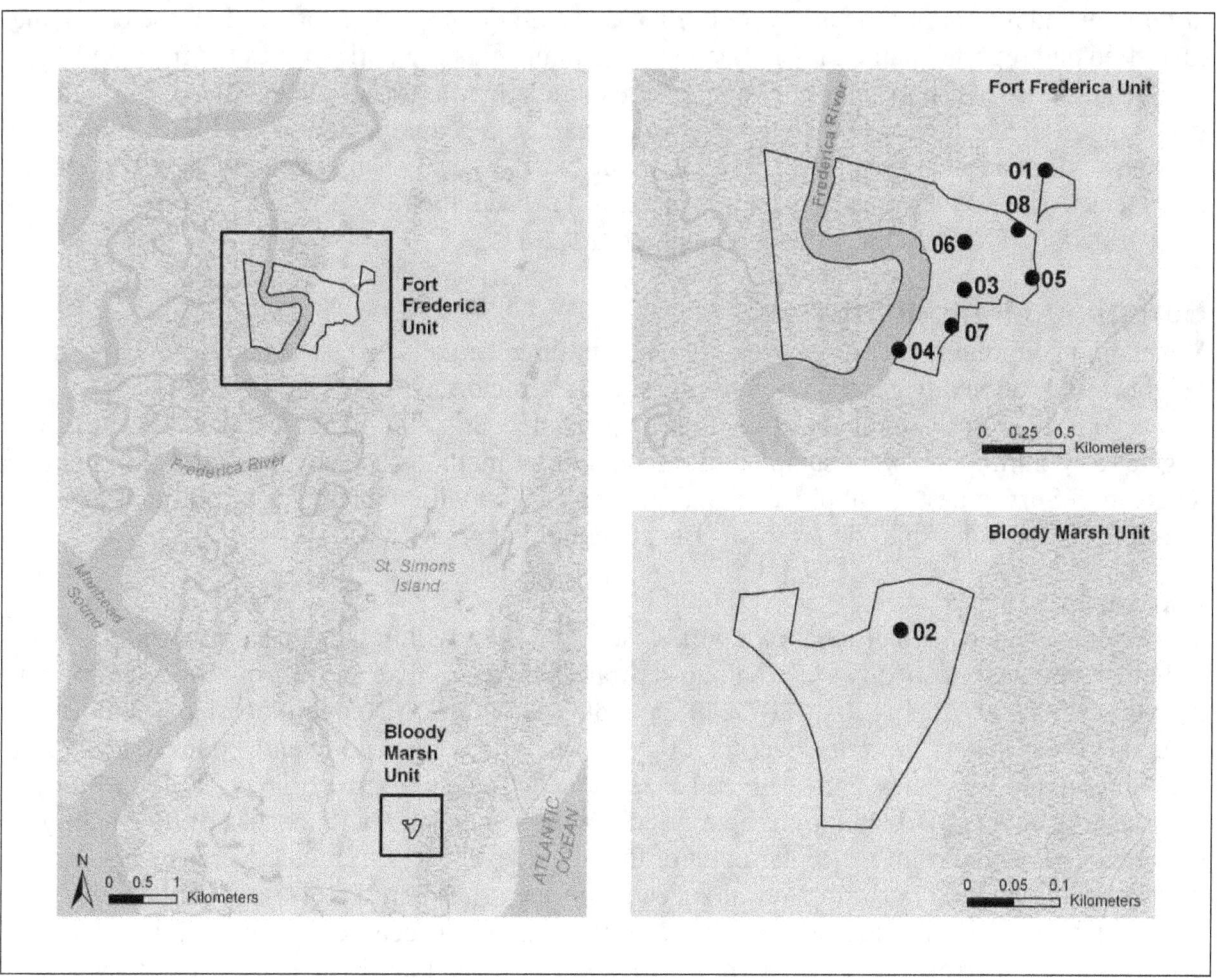

Figure 2. Spatially-balanced random sampling locations at Fort Frederica National Monument, 2009.

Taxonomic Standards

Species nomenclature for this report follow the current NPSpecies database accessible through the Integration of Resource Management Applications (IRMA) portal (https://irma.nps.gov/App/Portal/Home), which represents the most recent updates from the Integrated Taxonomic Information System (ITIS; http://www.itis.gov). Standards used for the botanical taxonomy in this report and for all work conducted by the Southeast Coast Network

(SECN) are in accordance with those set forth in by ITIS
(http://irma.nps.gov/content/help/taxonomy/FAQ.aspx).

Occasionally, if the available characteristics of a plant did not facilitate identification to genus, species, variety, or subspecies, the lowest level of taxonomy identifiable (i.e., the most refined) was used. For example, species of *Dicanthelium* are extremely difficult to identify to species when they lack floral or fruiting structures. In this case, the specimen may only be identified to genus as *Dicanthelium* sp. In the event that a species has more than one variety or subspecies that occurs for a park and the specific variety or subspecies cannot be identified in the field, only the genus and species name were used. For example, several varieties of *Pteridium aquilinum* are known. If for some reason the observer was only able to identify the plant as *Pteridium aquilinum* and not further to variety, only *Pteridium aquilinum* was reported. In these cases, the identified and reported name may not be included in the existing park species list from NPSpecies, only the sub-species or varieties are included in the park species list. Because the genus or species is already known to occur in the park, the general taxonomy will not appear in the "new vascular plant species" (Table 2). In the event a family name, generic name, or genera and species name only (no variety, subspecies, etc.) is used, the most recent taxonomy represented in ITIS is used for these general terms.

Sampling Methodology

Vegetation community measures were divided into three strata based upon diameter at breast height (DBH) of woody species: canopy, shrub, and groundcover. Any non-woody (i.e., herbaceous) species was considered part of the groundcover stratum. Within each stratum, vegetation communities were sampled using a hybrid of methods used by the North Carolina Vegetation Survey nested-subplot design (Peet et al. 1998) within a circular plot similar to the Forest Inventory and Analysis protocol (Bechtold and Patterson 2005).

Plot Layout

The layout consisted of a circular plot with a radius of 15 m within the 0.5-ha macroplot. Subplots were systematically placed along six transects that radiated out from the center point at azimuths of 0°/360°, 60°, 120°, 180°, 240°, and 300° (Figure 3). To avoid overlap, subplots originated four meters from the macroplot (i.e., 0.5-ha grid) center point and extended away from the center point. Five measures were collected in the nested subplots within each plot: canopy cover, shrub cover, DBH, canopy-species seedling frequency, and herbaceous cover. Canopy cover was measured from the center point of the 0.5-ha macroplot. Shrub coverage was measured in two 2 × 4 m shrub plots along each transect. The shrub plots were further subdivided into 2 × 2 m subplots to improve cover-estimation accuracy and precision because cover-estimation error increases with plot size (solid gray shading, Figure 3). Groundcover coverage, groundcover nested frequency, and seedling frequency was measured in two 1 × 1 m groundcover plots (solid black shading, Figure 3) along each transect. Canopy species DBH was measured in three sections, each representing 1/3 of the total circular plot (hashed gray shading, Figure 3).

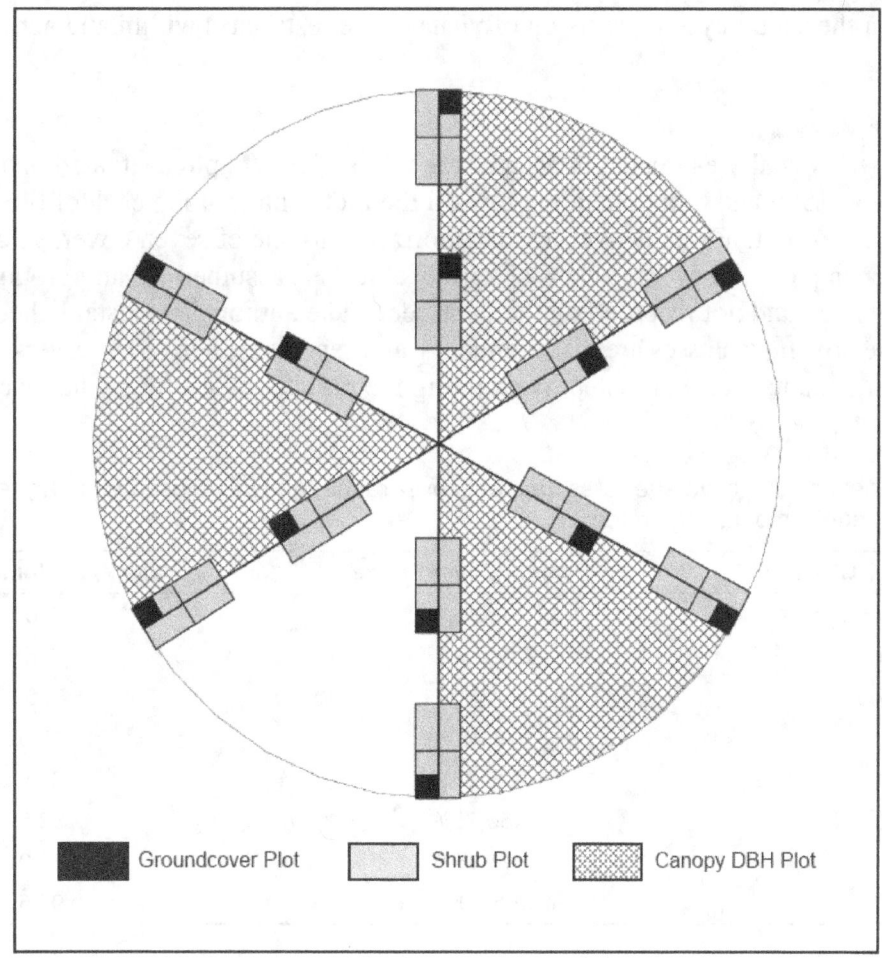

Figure 3. Southeast Coast Network vegetation-community monitoring plot layout.

Canopy Measures

Absolute canopy cover was estimated in the four cardinal directions with a concave spherical densiometer placed on a 1.1-m tall tripod at the plot center. Canopy cover reported is the mean of three observers across the four cardinal directions. The circular plot was subdivided into six sections occurring between the 0–60°, 120–180°, and 240–300° compass transects of the circular plot. Diameter at breast height (i.e., 1.37 m above the ground) was measured to the nearest millimeter for all trees (identified by species) with a diameter greater than or equal to 4 cm that occur within the 0–60°, 120–180°, and 240–300° section.

Shrub Measures

Shrub cover of all shrub species was visually estimated for each of the twelve 2 × 4 m plots. A common source of error in visual estimation of vegetation cover is that as plot size increases, cover-estimation error increases. Each shrub plot was therefore sub-divided into two 2 × 2 m subplots. The plots are situated at 15 m and 8 m (extending toward the plot center) along each of the transect lines of the circular plot. Shrub cover was categorized into one of seven coverage classes (Table 1) for each subplot. A coverage class of zero (Table 1) is assumed for any shrub species not detected and not recorded on the datasheet. The measurements of subplots were combined by averaging the midpoint for the coverage class in the two shrub subplots resulting in a total shrub cover estimate for the 2 × 4 m plot. The authors have established consistent performance in the accuracy and precision of visual-cover estimates within and across observers in plots this size.

Groundcover Measures

Groundcover was visually estimated in each of the twelve 1 × 1 m plots situated on the clockwise side at 15 m and 8 m (extending toward the plot center) along each of the transect lines of the circular plot. Groundcover was categorized into one of seven coverage classes (Table 1) for each plot. A coverage class of zero (Table 1) is assumed for any groundcover species not detected and not recorded on the datasheet. The authors have established through trials that these coverage classes are discriminatory and repeatable across observers. Canopy-species seedling counts were estimated by counting the number of seedlings that occur in each of the 1 × 1 m plots.

Table 1. Cover estimation coverage class, percent cover range, and value used for analyses for SECN vegetation-community monitoring protocol.

Coverage Class	Percent Cover Range	Value Used for Analyses
0	0%	0.0
1	Trace (<1%)	0.5
2	1-5%	2.5
3	5-25%	15.0
4	25-50%	37.5
5	50-75%	62.5
6	75-95%	85.0
7	95-100%	97.5

Data Analysis

Because this is the first year of this protocol's implementation at the Monument, only the status of the elements presented in the aforementioned monitoring objective are determined; except diversity and distribution. The data in this report are presented by plot and pooled across plots. Sampling locations are presented in Figure 2 and summaries by plot are presented in Tables 3–9.

Summaries include (a) new species detected (Table 2),(b) canopy cover (Table 3), (c) canopy species size (Table 4), (d) seedling frequency (Table 5), (e) shrub species relative cover and frequency (Table 6), shrub species absolute cover and frequency (Table 7), (f) groundcover relative cover and frequency (Table 8), (g) groundcover absolute cover and frequency (Table 9), and (h) species detected (Appendix A).

Findings

We detected 66 species, subspecies, and varieties during this monitoring effort (Appendix A), including 20 new species, subspecies, and varieties not previously known to occur at the Monument (Table 2).

Table 2. New vascular plant species detected at Fort Frederica National Monument during 2009 monitoring efforts and recommended NPSpecies classifications.

Species	Abundance	Nativity	Pest	Management Priority	Exploitation Concerns
Axonopus furcatus	Unknown	Native	No	No	No
Eremochloa ophiuroides	Unknown	Exo ic	No	No	No
Euthamia minor	Unknown	Native	No	No	No
Galium aparine	Unknown	Native	No	No	No
Gelsemium sempervirens	Unknown	Native	No	No	No
Gordonia lasianthus	Unknown	Native	No	No	No
Ilex cassine	Unknown	Native	No	No	No
Lyonia ferruginea	Unknown	Native	No	No	No
Lyonia lucida	Unknown	Native	No	No	No
Magnolia grandiflora	Unknown	Native	No	No	No
Nyssa sylvatica var. biflora	Unknown	Native	No	No	No
Osmanthus americanus	Unknown	Native	No	No	No
Paspalum notatum	Unknown	Exo ic	No	No	No
Persea palustris	Unknown	Native	No	No	No
Quercus geminata	Unknown	Native	No	No	No
Quercus laurifolia	Unknown	Native	No	No	No
Sideroxylon reclinatum	Unknown	Native	No	No	No
Smilax laurifolia	Unknown	Native	No	No	No
Sporobolus indicus	Unknown	Native	No	No	No

Measures of Community Structure

Absolute canopy cover was variable across the all sampling locations at the park ($\bar{x}$ = 76.8%, SD = 21.08; Table 3). Virginia live oak (*Quercus virginiana*) had the largest average DBH ($\bar{x}$ = 82.77 cm, SD = 13.26) of any species (Table 4). A single specimen of the non-native invasive Chinese privet (*Ligustrum sinense*) had a DBH of 5.30 cm (Table 4). A single live redbay DBH was 5.8 cm, and standing dead redbay DBH averaged 11.2 cm (n=2, SD=2.26; Table 4). Redbay seedlings were estimated at 0.02/m^2 (Table 5). The most frequently detected seedling was yaupon holly (*Ilex vomitoria*) (4.18/m^2). Yaupon holly, wax myrtle (*Morella cerifera*), and laurel oak (*Quercus laurifolia*) were the most frequently occurring shrub species at the park (f = 71.43). Waxmyrtle had the highest relative cover of all other shrub species ($\bar{x}$ = 23.77%, SD = 23.75), followed by yaupon holly ($\bar{x}$ = 23.13%, SD = 17.01), and saw palmetto (*Serenoa repens*) ($\bar{x}$ = 12.49%, SD = 25.94; Table 6). Yaupon holly had the highest absolute cover ($\bar{x}$ = 11.82%, SD = 11.45) followed by saw palmetto ($\bar{x}$ = 11.46%, SD = 26.97) and wax myrtle ($\bar{x}$ = 8.59%, SD = 7.71; Table 7). Camphortree occurred in the shrub stratum in approximately 14% of the sampling locations and had an average relative cover of 0.02% (SD = 0.06) and 1.11% (SD=2.94) (Table 6), and an average absolute cover of 0.01% (SD=0.04; Table 7). Chinese privet (*Ligustrum sinense*) also occurred in the shrub stratum in approximately 14% of the sampling locations and had an average relative cover 1.11% (SD=2.94; Table 6), and an average absolute cover of 0.46% (SD=1.22; Table 7). Redbay occurred in the shrub stratum in approximately 43% of sampling locations (Table 6). Yaupon holly had the highest absolute cover in the shrub stratum at the park ($\bar{x}$ = 11.82%, SD = 11.45), followed by saw palmetto ($\bar{x}$ = 11.46%, SD = 26.97; Table 7). Yaupon holly and wax myrtle were the most frequently occurring species (62.5%) in the groundcover stratum, (Table 8). Yaupon holly had the highest relative cover in the groundcover stratum ($\bar{x}$ =12.88%, SD = 20.73; Table 8). Bahiagrass (*Paspalum notatum*) had the highest absolute cover in the groundcover stratum ($\bar{x}$, = 6.43%, SD = 18.11; Table 9).

Table 3. Average canopy cover in vegetation monitoring sampling locations at Fort Frederica National Monument, 2009.

Site	Average Canopy Cover	Standard Deviation
1	85	
2	74.75	2.6
3	86.92	3.21
4	85	2.18
5	82.5	1.56
6	25.67	4.4
7	86.33	1.38
8	88.25	1.56
Park Average	**76.8**	**21.08**

Table 4. Average canopy species size, measured as diameter (cm) at breast height (DBH) for species sampled in vegetation monitoring sampling locations at Fort Frederica National Monument, 2009. Numbers in parentheses indicate the number of individual trees measured within each plot.

Species	Average	Standard Deviation	Sampling Point							
			1	2	3	4	5	6	7	8
Acer rubrum	9.4		9.40 (1)							
Cephalanthus occidentalis	7.1	1.35					7.10 (1)			
Cercis canadensis	5.9				5.90 (4)					
Gordonia lasianthus	20.4	10.56	20.40 (6)							
Ilex cassine	5.6			5.60 (1)						
Ilex opaca	11.17	5.32	14.15 (2)						5.20 (1)	
Ilex vomitoria	5.32	1.19		4.54 (5)	5.86 (7)				5.08 (6)	6.10 (2)
Juniperus virginiana var. silicicola	13.8	8.13				13.80 (5)				
Ligustrum sinense	5.3				5.30 (1)					
Liquidambar styraciflua	20.7	13.65			17.73 (8)		20.13 (3)		14.80 (1)	36.40 (2)
Lyonia ferruginea	5.73	2.35	5.73 (4)							
Magnolia grandiflora	16.07	12.06		29.80 (1)			7.20 (1)		11.20 (1)	
Morus rubra	5.1	0.28		5.10 (2)						
Morella cerifera	4.1								4.10 (1)	
Nyssa sylvatica var. biflora	32.1	15.56	32.10 (2)							
Nyssa sylvatica	10.7	7.5				10.70 (2)				
Persea borbonia	5.8		5.80 (1)							
Persea palustris	5		5.00 (1)							
Pinus taeda	44.53	14.67	32.82 (6)		48.28 (4)				49.67 (3)	49.53 (8)
Prunus caroliniana	8.01	2.42		8.01 (28)						
Prunus serotina	13.8								13.80 (1)	
Quercus geminata	48.7							48.70 (1)		
Quercus laurifolia	18.05	13.26		13.51 (18)	21.57 (3)	21.01 (13)			20.44 (10)	22.50 (2)
Quercus nigra	17.58	9.89	24.40 (9)				14.28 (8)			14.09 (10)
Quercus virginiana	82.77	41.15		82.77 (3)						
Rhus copallinum	6.7				6.70 (1)					
Sabal palmetto	27.45	5.02		27.45 (2)						
Symplocos tinctoria	4.5								4.50 (1)	
Vaccinium arboreum	4.4	0.57		4.00 (1)		4.80 (1)				
Vaccinium conymbosum	4.4					4.40 (1)				
Vitis rotundifolia	12.8				12.80 (1)					
Dead										
Ilex sp.	5.4			5.40 (1)						
Ilex vomitoria	5.7								5.70 (1)	
Juniperus virginiana var. silicicola	11.95	0.07				11.95 (2)				
Ligustrum sinense	8.4				8.40 (1)					
Persea borbonia	11.2	2.26			9.60 (1)					12.80 (1)
Pinus sp.	11.1						11.10 (1)			
Pinus taeda	29.3									29.30 (1)
Prunus caroliniana	6.9	0.99		6.90 (2)						
Prunus serotina	9.2									9.20 (1)
Quercus laurifolia	6.3			6.30 (1)						

11

Table 4. Continued.

Species	Average	Standard Deviation	Sampling Point							
			1	2	3	4	5	6	7	8
Quercus nigra	8.6						8.60 (1)			
Quercus sp.	13.62	3.71		14.20 (1)	13.80 (1)	16.90 (2)	10.60 (1)			9.30 (1)
Unidentified										
Magnoliopsida	4.9			4.60 (1)					5.20 (1)	

Table 5. Seedling frequency for canopy and shrub species in vegetation monitoring sampling locations at Fort Frederica National Monument, 2009.

Species	Total Seedlings	Seedlings/m2	Std Dev	Sampling Point							
				1	2	3	4	5	6	7	8
Acer rubrum	15	0.16	0.44					1.25			
Callicarpa americana	2	0.02	0.06		0.17						
Cinnamomum camphora	2	0.02	0.06							0.17	
Ilex vomitoria	401	4.18	8.08		23.67	0.92	3.33			4.92	0.58
Ligustrum sinense	1	0.01	0.03			0.08					
Liquidambar styraciflua	3	0.03	0.09					0.25			
Lyonia lucida	3	0.03	0.09	0.25							
Morella cerifera	13	0.14	0.13			0.25	0.08	0.33		0.25	0.17
Parthenocissus quinquefolia	0	0	0							0.00	
Persea borbonia	2	0.02	0.06	0.17							
Pinus taeda	14	0.15	0.32				0.08	0.92			0.17
Prunus caroliniana	52	0.54	1.5		4.25					0.08	
Quercus geminata	9	0.09	0.27						0.75		
Quercus laurifolia	136	1.42	2.15	0.42		4.67	0.25	0.25		5.08	0.67
Quercus nigra	16	0.17	0.35	0.08				0.25			1.00
Quercus sp.	41	0.43	1.14		3.25			0.17			
Sabal palmetto	2	0.02	0.06		0.17						
Serenoa repens	4	0.04	0.08				0.17				
Smilax sp.	1	0.01	0.03	0.08							
Symplocos tinctoria	2	0.02	0.04	0.08						0.08	
Vaccinium corymbosum	3	0.03	0.06				0.08			0.17	

Table 6. Percent of vegetation cover (relative cover) and frequency of occurrence of shrub species in vegetation monitoring sampling locations at Fort Frederica National Monument, 2009.

Species	Frequency	Average	Standard Deviation	1	2	3	4	5	6	7	8
							Sampling Point				
Aralia spinosa	14.29	0.9	2.37			6.28					
Callicarpa americana	28.57	0.43	0.84		0.79					2.23	
Celtis laevigata	14.29	0.02	0.05		0.13						
Cercis canadensis	14.29	1.44	3.8			10.05					
Cinnamomum camphora	14.29	0.02	0.06							0.17	
Diospyros virginiana	14.29	0	0.01		0.03						
Ilex glabra	14.29	0.31	0.81					2.15			
Ilex opaca	14.29	0.37	0.97							2.57	
Ilex vomitoria	71.43	23.13	17.01		38.56	26.13	36.75			38.36	22.11
Ligustrum sinense	14.29	1.11	2.94			7.79					
Liquidambar styraciflua	14.29	0.31	0.81					2.15			
Lyonia ferruginea	14.29	0.9	2.38	6.31							
Lyonia lucida	14.29	1.53	4.04	10.68							
Magnolia grandiflora	28.57	0.07	0.13		0.13					0.34	
Morella cerifera	71.43	23.77	23.75			28.39	5.30	49.82		24.32	58.60
Osmanthus americanus	14.29	0.13	0.35		0.92						
Persea borbonia	42.86	2.16	3.15			1.76				6.68	6.67
Persea palustris	28.57	3.11	6.44	4.58				17.20			
Pinus taeda	28.57	2.99	5.49				6.95	13.98			
Prunus caroliniana	14.29	1.87	4.94		13.07						
Quercus laurifolia	71.43	4.75	6.34		16.58		1.99	0.36		10.10	4.21
Quercus nigra	42.86	1.3	2.03	0.61				4.30			4.21
Quercus sp	14.29	1.04	2.75		7.26	3.02					
Rhus copallinum	14.29	0.43	1.14								
Sabal palmetto	28.57	4.17	10.13		27.07			2.15			
Serenoa repens	57.14	12.49	25.94	70.79	5.28		9.27				2.11
Sideroxylon reclinatum	14.29	0.11	0.3		0.79						
Symplocos tinctoria	42.86	0.77	1	1.22						2.05	2.11
Vaccinium arboreum	42.86	1.87	2.73	1.55	5.94		5.63				
Vaccinium corymbosum	57.14	7.67	12.57	4.27			34.11	2.15		13.18	
Yucca aloifolia	14.29	0.82	2.17					5.73			

Table 7. Percent area covered (absolute cover) and frequency of occurrence of shrub species sampled in vegetation monitoring sampling locations at Fort Frederica National Monument, 2009.

Species	Frequency	Average	Standard Deviation	Sampling Point							
				1	2	3	4	5	6	7	8
Aralia spinosa	14.29	0.37	0.98			2.60					
Callicarpa americana	28.57	0.28	0.53		0.63					1.35	
Celtis laevigata	14.29	0.01	0.04		0.10						
Cercis canadensis	14.29	0.6	1.57			4.17					
Cinnamomum camphora	14.29	0.01	0.04							0.10	
Diospyros virginiana	14.29	0	0.01		0.02						
Ilex glabra	14.29	0.09	0.24					0.63			
Ilex opaca	14.29	0.22	0.59							1.56	
Ilex vomitoria	71.43	11.82	11.45		30.42	10.83	11.56			23.33	6.56
Ligustrum sinense	14.29	0.46	1.22			3.23					
Liquidambar styraciflua	14.29	0.09	0.24					0.63			
Lyonia ferruginea	14.29	0.92	2.44	6.46							
Lyonia lucida	14.29	1.56	4.13	10.94							
Magnolia grandiflora	28.57	0.04	0.08		0.10					0.21	
Morella cerifera	71.43	8.59	7.71			11.77	1.67	14.48		14.79	17.40
Osmanthus americanus	14.29	0.1	0.28		0.73						
Persea borbonia	42.86	0.97	1.55			0.73				4.06	1.98
Persea palustris	28.57	1.38	2.37	4.69				5.00			
Pinus taeda	28.57	0.89	1.62				2.19	4.06			
Prunus caroliniana	14.29	1.47	3.9		10.31						
Quercus laurifolia	71.43	2.14	3.02			6.88	0.63	0.10		6.15	1.25
Quercus nigra	42.86	0.45	0.59	0.63				1.25			1.25
Quercus sp.	14.29	0.82	2.17		5.73						
Rhus copallinum	14.29	0.18	0.47			1.25					
Sabal palmetto	28.57	3.14	8.04		21.35			0.63			
Serenoa repens	57.14	11.46	26.97	72.50	4.17		2.92				0.63
Sideroxylon recinatum	14.29	0.09	0.24		0.63						
Symplocos tinctoria	42.86	0.45	0.59	1.25						1.25	0.63
Vaccinium arboreum	42.86	1.15	1.75	1.58	4.69		1.77				
Vaccinium corymbosum	57.14	3.39	4.44	4.38			10.73	0.63		8.02	
Yucca aloifolia	14.29	0.24	0.63					1.67			

15

Table 8. Percent of vegetation cover (relative cover) and frequency of occurrence of groundcover species in vegetation monitoring sampling locations at Fort Frederica National Monument, 2009

Species	Frequency	Average	Standard Deviation	Sampling Point							
				1	2	3	4	5	6	7	8
Acer rubrum	12.5	0.49	1.4					3.96			
Ampelopsis arborea	12.5	0.08	0.22			0.62					
Axonopus furcatus	12.5	0.68	1.91						5.41		
Bignonia capreolata	25	0.83	1.54			3.73					2.88
Callicarpa americana	12.5	0.08	0.23		0.66						
Cinnamomum camphora	12.5	0.04	0.13							0.36	
Cyperus sp.	12.5	0	0.01						0.03		
Elephantopus sp.	25	0.57	1.39		3.97	0.62					
Eremochloa ophiuroides	25	2.49	5.7			3.73			16.22		
Eupatorium capillifolium	12.5	0.12	0.33						0.93		
Euthamia minor	12.5	0	0.01						0.03		
Galium aparine	25	0.17	0.48			1.37			0.03		
Gelsemium sempervirens	25	0.58	1.31			3.73				0.9	
Ilex vomitoria	62.5	12.88	20.73		55.1	4.35	6.55			35.13	1.94
Ligustrum sinense	12.5	0.48	1.36			3.85					
Liquidambar styraciflua	12.5	0.99	2.8					7.92			
Lyonia lucida	12.5	0.05	0.14	0.39							
Morella cerifera	62.5	0.66	0.91			0.75	0.34	2.64		1.25	0.31
Optismenus hirtellus	12.5	0.08	0.22			0.62					
Osmunda cinnamomea	25	1.2	2.78	1.67				7.92			
Oxalis stricta	25	0.51	1.31			3.73			0.39		
Panicum sp.	12.5	1.04	2.94			8.32					
Parthenocissus quinquefolia	50	2.86	5.29		0.66	14.29				7.53	0.38
Paspalum notatum	25	4.69	13.03			0.62			36.94		
Persea borbonia	12.5	0.01	0.02	0.06							
Phyla nodiflora	12.5	1.84	5.2						14.71		
Pinus taeda	37.5	1.38	3.82				0.07	10.82		0.13	
Prunus caroliniana	25	1.94	5.42		15.36						
Pteridium aquilinum	12.5	0.16	0.47					1.32			
Quercus geminata	12.5	0.11	0.32								
Quercus laurifolia	75	6.18	10.76	0.22		19.5	0.14	1.58	0.9	27.06	
Quercus nigra	37.5	0.56	1.08	0.06				1.58			2.88
Quercus sp.	25	1.87	4.78		13.64			1.32			
Rubus sp.	37.5	0.18	0.32			0.75			0.03		0.63
Ruella sp.	12.5	0.02	0.05						0.15		
Sabal palmetto	12.5	0.08	0.23		0.66						
Scleria triglomerata	12.5	0.08	0.23		0.66						
Serenoa repens	25	0.08	0.15				0.34				
Smilax bona-nox	37.5	0.42	0.78		1.32		0.07			1.97	
Smilax laurifolia	37.5	0.26	0.69						0.03	1.97	0.06
Smilax sp.	37.5	0.04	0.05	0.11		0.12					0.06
Sporobolus indicus	12.5	0	0.01						0.03		

Table 8. Continued.

Species	Frequency	Average	Standard Deviation	1	2	3	4	5	6	7	8
							Sampling Point				
Symplocos tinctoria	25	0.03	0.06	0.06						0.18	
Taraxacum officinale	12.5	0.12	0.33						0.93		
Toxicodendron radicans	37.5	2.87	5.59			14.91		7.92			0.13
Tradescantia ohiensis	12.5	0	0.01						0.03		
Vaccinium corymbosum	25	0.27	0.63				0.34			1.79	
Viola sp.	12.5	0.02	0.04			0.12					
Vitis rotundifolia	50	3.75	7.44		3.97	0.62				21.68	3.75
Woodwardia areolata	12.5	0.03	0.09					0.26			
Unidentified											
Tracheobionta	12.5	0.5	1.4		3.97						
Asteraceae	12.5	0.08	0.22			0.62					
Fabaceae	25	1.17	3.29			9.32			0.03		
Filicopsida	12.5	0.47	1.32			3.73					
Lamiaceae	12.5	0	0.01						0.03		
Poaceae	12.5	0.11	0.32						0.9		
Ground Condition											
Bare ground	25	6.34	17.57				49.83		0.9		
Leaf litter or duff	62.5	29.42	38.31	97.45			40.27	1.32	21.32		75
Open water	12.5	6.43	18.19					51.45			
Tree stump	12.5	1.33	3.76								10.63
Upland non-vascular plants or lichens	12.5	0.26	0.72				2.05				

Table 9. Percent area covered (absolute cover) and frequency of occurrence by groundcover species sampled in vegetation monitoring sampling locations at Fort Frederica National Monument, 2009.

Species	Frequency	Average	Standard Deviation	Sampling Point							
				1	2	3	4	5	6	7	8
Acer rubrum	12.5	0.08	0.22					0.63			
Ampelopsis arborea	12.5	0.03	0.07			0.21					
Axonopus furcatus	12.5	0.94	2.65						7.5		
Bignonia capreolata	25	0.4	0.75			1.25					1.92
Callicarpa americana	12.5	0.03	0.07		0.21						
Cinnamomum camphora	12.5	0.01	0.03							0.08	
Cyperus sp.	12.5	0.01	0.01						0.04		
Elephantopus sp.	25	0.18	0.44		1.25	0.21					
Eremochloa ophiuroides	25	2.97	7.9			1.25			22.5		
Eupatorium capillifolium	12.5	0.16	0.46						1.29		
Euthamia minor	12.5	0.01	0.01						0.04		
Galium aparine	25	0.06	0.16			0.46			0.04		
Gelsemium sempervirens	25	0.18	0.44			1.25				0.21	
Ilex vomitoria	62.5	4.03	6.06		17.33	1.46	4			8.17	1.29
Ligustrum sinense	12.5	0.16	0.46			1.29					
Liquidambar styraciflua	12.5	0.16	0.44					1.25			
Lyonia lucida	12.5	0.04	0.1	0.29							
Morella cerifera	62.5	0.17	0.16			0.25	0.21	0.42		0.29	0.21
Oplismenus hirtellus	12.5	0.03	0.07			0.21					
Osmunda cinnamomea	25	0.31	0.58	1.25				1.25			
Oxalis stricta	25	0.22	0.46			1.25			0.54		
Panicum sp	12.5	0.35	0.99			2.79					
Parthenocissus quinquefolia	50	0.88	1.69		0.21	4.79				1.75	0.25
Paspalum notatum	25	6.43	18.11		0.21				51.25		
Persea borbonia	12.5	0.01	0.01	0.04							
Phyla nodiflora	12.5	2.55	7.22						20.42		
Pinus taeda	37.5	0.23	0.6				0.04	1.71		0.04	0.08
Prunus caroliniana	25	0.61	1.71		4.83					0.04	
Pteridium aquilinum	12.5	0.03	0.07					0.21			
Quercus geminata	12.5	0.16	0.44						1.25		
Quercus laurifolia	75	1.74	2.89	0.17		6.54	0.08	0.25		6.29	0.63
Quercus nigra	37.5	0.28	0.67	0.04				0.25			1.92
Quercus sp.	25	0.56	1.51		4.29			0.21			
Rubus sp.	37.5	0.09	0.16			0.25			0.04		0.42
Ruella sp.	12.5	0.03	0.07						0.21		
Sabal palmetto	12.5	0.03	0.07		0.21						
Scleria triglomerata	12.5	0.03	0.07		0.21						
Serenoa repens	25	0.05	0.1				0.21				0.21
Smilax bona-nox	37.5	0.11	0.2		0.42		0.04			0.46	
Smilax laurifolia	37.5	0.07	0.16			0.04			0.04	0.46	0.04
Smilax sp.	37.5	0.02	0.03	0.08		0.04					0.04
Sporobolus indicus	12.5	0.01	0.01						0.04		

Table 9. Continued.

Species	Frequency	Average	Standard Deviation	Sampling Point							
				1	2	3	4	5	6	7	8
Symplocos tinctoria	25	0.01	0.02							0.04	
Taraxacum officinale	12.5	0.16	0.46						1.29		
Toxicodendron radicans	37.5	0.79	1.75			5		1.25			0.08
Tradescantia ohiensis	12.5	0.01	0.01						0.04		
Vaccinium corymbosum	25	0.08	0.16				0.21			0.42	
Viola sp.	12.5	0.01	0.01			0.04					
Vitis rotundifolia	50	1.13	1.82		1.25	0.21				5.04	2.5
Woodwardia areolata	12.5	0.01	0.01					0.04			
Unidentified											
Tracheobionta	12.5	0.16	0.44		1.25						
Asteraceae	12.5	0.03	0.07			0.21					
Fabaceae	25	0.4	1.1			3.13			0.04		
Filicopsida	12.5	0.16	0.44			1.25					
Lamiaceae	12.5	0.01	0.01						0.04		
Poaceae	12.5	0.16	0.44						1.25		
Ground Condition											
Bare ground	25	3.96	10.7	73.13			30.42		1.25		
Leaf litter or duff	62.5	22.19	27.75				24.58	0.21	29.58		50
Open water	12.5	1.02	2.87					8.13			
Tree stump	12.5	0.89	2.5								7.08
Upland non-vascular plants or lichens	12.5	0.16	0.44				1.25				

Literature Cited

Bechtold, W. A. and P. L. Patterson, (eds.). 2005. The enhanced forest inventory and analysis program — national sampling design and estimation procedures. General Technical Report SRS-80. USDA Forest Service, Southern Research Station, Asheville, NC. 85 pp.

Bratton, S. P. 1983. The vegetation history of Fort Frederica, Saint Simons Island, Georgia. Research/Resource Management Report SER-66. USDI National Park Service. 29pp.

Byrne, M. W. 2009. Sampling-point generation for SECN monitoring protocols: Generating a spatially-balanced random sample with the RRQRR tool in ArcGIS 9.1. Draft Standard Operating Procedure Version 1.0, last updated March 2009.

Byrne, M. W., S. L. Corbett, E. Thompson, and C. J. Wright. *In preparation*. Draft vegetation community monitoring in Southeast Coast Network parks. USDI National Park Service, Southeast Coast Network, Atlanta, GA, USA.

DeVivo, J. C., C. J. Wright, M. W. Byrne, E. DiDonato, and T. Curtis. 2008. Vital signs monitoring in the Southeast Coast Inventory & Monitoring Network. Natural Resource Report NPS/SECN/NRR—2008/061. USDI National Park Service, Fort Collins, CO, USA.

Federal Geographic Data Committee. 2008. National vegetation classification standard, version 2. FGDC-STD-005-2008. Available online: http://www.fgdc.gov/standards/project/FGDC-standards-projects/vegetation.

Foster, D. R., G. Motzkin, and B. Slater. 1998. Land-use history as long-term broad-scale disturbance: regional forest dynamics in central New England. Ecosystems: 1:96-119.

Fraedrich S. W., T. C. Harrington, R. J. Rabaglia, M. D. Ulyshen, A. E. Mayfield III, J. L. Hanula, J. M. Eickwort, and D. R. Miller. 2008. A fungal symbiont of the redbay ambrosia beetle causes a lethal wilt in redbay and other Lauraceae in the southeastern United States. Plant Disease 92:215–224.

Haack, R. A. 2006. Exotic bark- and wood-boring Coleoptera in the United States: Recent establishments and interceptions. Canadian Journal of Forest Research 36:269-288.

NPSpecies - The National Park Service Biodiversity Database. Secure online version. https://science1.nature.nps.gov/npspecies/web/main/start (Park list: accessed 1/13/2011).

Peet R. K., T. R. Wentworth, and P. S White. 1998. A flexible, multipurpose method for recording vegetation composition and structure. Castanea 63:262-274.

Rabaglia, R. 2003. Xyleborus glabratus. Online record, URL: http://spfnic.fs.fed.us/exfor/data/pestreports.cfm?pestidval=148&langdisplay=english (Accessed 2/14/2012).

Theobald, D. M., D. L. Stevens, D. White, N. S. Urquhart, A. R. Olsen, and J. B. Norman. 2007. Using GIS to generate spatially balanced random survey designs for natural resource applications Environmental Management 40:134-146.

Turner, II, B. L., W. C. Clark, R. W. Kates, J. F. Richards, J. T. Mathews, and W. B. Meyer, (eds.). 1990. The earth as transformed by human action: Global and regional changes in the biosphere over the past 300 years. Cambridge University Press, Cambridge, UK.

Appendix A. Plant species known to occur at Fort Frederica National Monument.

Table A-1. Vascular plant species known occur at Fort Frederica National Monument (NPSpecies 2011) and species detected during 2009 monitoring efforts.

Family	Species	NPSpecies	This Study
Acanthaceae	*Ruellia caroliniensis*	X	
Aceraceae	*Acer rubrum*	X	X
Agavaceae	*Yucca aloifolia*	X	X
Anacardiaceae	*Rhus copallinum*	X	X
Anacardiaceae	*Toxicodendron radicans*	X	X
Annonaceae	*Asimina parviflora*	X	
Apiaceae	*Chaerophyllum tainturieri*	X	
Apiaceae	*Hydrocotyle bonariensis*	X	
Apiaceae	*Hydrocotyle umbellata*	X	
Apiaceae	*Ptilimnium capillaceum*	X	
Apiaceae	*Sanicula canadensis*	X	
Apocynaceae	*Nerium oleander*	X	
Aquifoliaceae	*Ilex cassine*		X
Aquifoliaceae	*Ilex glabra*	X	X
Aquifoliaceae	*Ilex myrtifolia*	X	
Aquifoliaceae	*Ilex opaca*	X	X
Aquifoliaceae	*Ilex vomitoria*	X	X
Araceae	*Arisaema dracontium*	X	
Araliaceae	*Aralia spinosa*	X	X
Arecaceae	*Sabal minor*	X	
Arecaceae	*Sabal palmetto*	X	X
Arecaceae	*Serenoa repens*	X	X
Asclepiadaceae	*Cynanchum angustifolium*	X	
Asteraceae	*Ambrosia artemisiifolia*	X	
Asteraceae	*Baccharis angustifolia*	X	
Asteraceae	*Baccharis halimifolia*	X	
Asteraceae	*Borrichia frutescens*	X	
Asteraceae	*Carphephorus odoratissimus*	X	
Asteraceae	*Cirsium horridulum var. horridulum*	X	
Asteraceae	*Cirsium nuttallii*	X	
Asteraceae	*Conyza bonariensis*	X	
Asteraceae	*Conyza canadensis*	X	
Asteraceae	*Conyza canadensis var. pusilla*	X	
Asteraceae	*Elephantopus elatus*	X	
Asteraceae	*Elephantopus nudatus*	X	
Asteraceae	*Erigeron quercifolius*	X	
Asteraceae	*Erigeron strigosus*	X	
Asteraceae	*Eupatorium capillifolium*	X	X
Asteraceae	*Euthamia minor*		X
Asteraceae	*Facelis retusa*	X	
Asteraceae	*Gamochaeta pensylvanica*	X	
Asteraceae	*Gamochaeta purpurea*	X	
Asteraceae	*Gnaphalium obtusifolium*	X	
Asteraceae	*Iva frutescens*	X	
Asteraceae	*Krigia virginica*	X	
Asteraceae	*Melanthera nivea*	X	

Table A-1. Continued.

Family	Species	NPSpecies	This Study
Asteraceae	*Mikania scandens*	X	
Asteraceae	*Pluchea rosea*	X	
Asteraceae	*Pyrrhopappus carolinianus var. georgianus*	X	
Asteraceae	*Solidago odora*	X	
Asteraceae	*Sonchus asper*	X	
Asteraceae	*Sonchus oleraceus*	X	
Asteraceae	*Symphyotrichum tenuifolium*	X	
Asteraceae	*Taraxacum officinale*	X	X
Asteraceae	*Verbesina occidentalis*	X	
Asteraceae	*Verbesina virginica*	X	
Asteraceae	*Youngia japonica*	X	
Bataceae	*Batis maritima*	X	
Bignoniaceae	*Bignonia capreolata*	X	X
Bignoniaceae	*Campsis radicans*	X	
Bignoniaceae	*Catalpa speciosa*	X	
Blechnaceae	*Woodwardia areolata*	X	X
Brassicaceae	*Cardamine hirsuta*	X	
Brassicaceae	*Lepidium virginicum*	X	
Brassicaceae	*Rorippa nasturtium-aquaticum*	X	
Bromeliaceae	*Tillandsia usneoides*	X	
Buddlejaceae	*Polypremum procumbens*	X	
Cactaceae	*Opuntia ficus-indica*	X	
Cactaceae	*Opuntia humifusa*	X	
Campanulaceae	*Specularia perfoliata*	X	
Caprifoliaceae	*Lonicera japonica*	X	
Caprifoliaceae	*Lonicera sempervirens*	X	
Caryophyllaceae	*Cerastium glomeratum*	X	
Caryophyllaceae	*Cerastium holosteoides var. vulgare*	X	
Caryophyllaceae	*Paronychia baldwinii ssp. riparia*	X	
Caryophyllaceae	*Spergularia salina*	X	
Caryophyllaceae	*Stellaria media*	X	
Chenopodiaceae	*Salicornia virginica*	X	
Cistaceae	*Helianthemum carolinianum*	X	
Cistaceae	*Helianthemum corymbosum*	X	
Cistaceae	*Lechea mucronata*	X	
Clusiaceae	*Hypericum cistifolium*	X	
Clusiaceae	*Hypericum crux-andreae*	X	
Clusiaceae	*Hypericum hypericoides*	X	
Clusiaceae	*Hypericum mutilum*	X	
Commelinaceae	*Tradescantia ohiensis*	X	X
Convolvulaceae	*Dichondra carolinensis*	X	
Convolvulaceae	*Ipomoea cordatotriloba var. cordatotriloba*	X	
Convolvulaceae	*Ipomoea sagittata*	X	
Cornaceae	*Cornus florida*	X	
Cupressaceae	*Juniperus virginiana var. silicicola*	X	X
Cycadaceae	*Cycas revoluta*	X	
Cyperaceae	*Carex longii*	X	
Cyperaceae	*Cyperus croceus*	X	
Cyperaceae	*Cyperus pseudovegetus*	X	
Cyperaceae	*Cyperus retrorsus*	X	
Cyperaceae	*Cyperus strigosus*	X	

Table A-1. Continued.

Family	Species	NPSpecies	This Study
Cyperaceae	*Eleocharis vivipara*	X	
Cyperaceae	*Fimbristylis thermalis*	X	
Cyperaceae	*Rhynchospora colorata*	X	
Cyperaceae	*Rhynchospora miliacea*	X	
Cyperaceae	*Scleria triglomerata*	X	X
Dennstaedtiaceae	*Pteridium aquilinum*	X	X
Ebenaceae	*Diospyros virginiana*	X	X
Ericaceae	*Lyonia ferruginea*		X
Ericaceae	*Lyonia lucida*		X
Ericaceae	*Vaccinium arboreum*	X	X
Ericaceae	*Vaccinium corymbosum*	X	X
Ericaceae	*Vaccinium elliottii*	X	
Ericaceae	*Vaccinium fuscatum*	X	
Euphorbiaceae	*Cnidoscolus stimulosus*	X	
Euphorbiaceae	*Croton willdenowii*	X	
Euphorbiaceae	*Triadica sebifera*	X	
Fabaceae	*Amorpha herbacea*	X	
Fabaceae	*Centrosema virginianum*	X	
Fabaceae	*Cercis canadensis*	X	X
Fabaceae	*Chamaecrista fasciculata var. fasciculata*	X	
Fabaceae	*Chamaecrista nictitans var. nictitans*	X	
Fabaceae	*Clitoria mariana*	X	
Fabaceae	*Desmodium incanum*	X	
Fabaceae	*Desmodium paniculatum*	X	
Fabaceae	*Desmodium tenuifolium*	X	
Fabaceae	*Erythrina herbacea*	X	
Fabaceae	*Galactia volubilis*	X	
Fabaceae	*Lespedeza hirta*	X	
Fabaceae	*Lespedeza X manniana*	X	
Fabaceae	*Medicago arabica*	X	
Fabaceae	*Medicago polymorpha*	X	
Fabaceae	*Robinia pseudoacacia*	X	
Fabaceae	*Sesbania punicea*	X	
Fabaceae	*Trifolium campestre*	X	
Fabaceae	*Trifolium carolinianum*	X	
Fabaceae	*Trifolium repens*	X	
Fabaceae	*Vicia angustifolia*	X	
Fabaceae	*Vicia caroliniana*	X	
Fabaceae	*Wisteria sinensis*	X	
Fagaceae	*Castanea pumila*	X	
Fagaceae	*Quercus austrina*	X	
Fagaceae	*Quercus geminata*		X
Fagaceae	*Quercus hemisphaerica*	X	
Fagaceae	*Quercus laurifolia*		X
Fagaceae	*Quercus nigra*	X	X
Fagaceae	*Quercus virginiana*	X	X
Geraniaceae	*Geranium carolinianum*	X	
Hamamelidaceae	*Liquidambar styraciflua*	X	X
Iridaceae	*Iris hexagona*	X	
Iridaceae	*Sisyrinchium rosulatum*	X	
Juglandaceae	*Carya glabra*	X	

Table A-1. Continued.

Family	Species	NPSpecies	This Study
Juglandaceae	*Carya illinoinensis*	X	
Juncaceae	*Juncus coriaceus*	X	
Juncaceae	*Juncus roemerianus*	X	
Lamiaceae	*Monarda clinopodia*	X	
Lamiaceae	*Salvia azurea*	X	
Lamiaceae	*Salvia coccinea*	X	
Lamiaceae	*Salvia lyrata*	X	
Lamiaceae	*Scutellaria elliptica*	X	
Lamiaceae	*Scutellaria incana*	X	
Lamiaceae	*Stachys floridana*	X	
Lamiaceae	*Teucrium canadense*	X	
Lauraceae	*Cinnamomum camphora*	X	X
Lauraceae	*Persea borbonia*	X	X
Lauraceae	*Persea palustris*		X
Lauraceae	*Sassafras albidum*	X	
Liliaceae	*Leucojum aestivum*	X	
Liliaceae	*Narcissus X medioluteus*	X	
Liliaceae	*Nothoscordum bivalve*	X	
Liliaceae	*Zephyranthes atamasca*	X	
Loganiaceae	*Gelsemium sempervirens*		X
Lythraceae	*Cuphea carthagenensis*	X	
Lythraceae	*Lagerstroemia indica*	X	
Magnoliaceae	*Magnolia grandiflora*		X
Magnoliaceae	*Magnolia virginiana*	X	
Malvaceae	*Sida rhombifolia*	X	
Melastomataceae	*Rhexia alifanus*	X	
Menispermaceae	*Cocculus carolinus*	X	
Molluginaceae	*Mollugo verticillata*	X	
Moraceae	*Ficus carica*	X	
Moraceae	*Maclura pomifera*	X	
Moraceae	*Morus rubra*	X	X
Myricaceae	*Morella cerifera*	X	X
Nyssaceae	*Nyssa syvatica var. biflora*		X
Nyssaceae	*Nyssa sylvatica*	X	X
Oleaceae	*Ligustrum amurense*	X	
Oleaceae	*Ligustrum japonicum*	X	
Oleaceae	*Ligustrum sinense*	X	X
Oleaceae	*Osmanthus americanus*		X
Onagraceae	*Gaura angustifolia*	X	
Orchidaceae	*Listera australis*	X	
Osmundaceae	*Osmunda cinnamomea*	X	X
Oxalidaceae	*Oxalis dillenii ssp. filipes*	X	
Oxalidaceae	*Oxalis rubra*	X	
Oxalidaceae	*Oxalis stricta*	X	X
Oxalidaceae	*Oxalis violacea*	X	
Papaveraceae	*Argemone albiflora*	X	
Passifloraceae	*Passiflora incarnata*	X	
Phytolaccaceae	*Phytolacca americana*	X	
Pinaceae	*Pinus taeda*	X	X
Pittosporaceae	*Pittosporum tobira*	X	
Plantaginaceae	*Plantago major*	X	

Table A-1. Continued.

Family	Species	NPSpecies	This Study
Plantaginaceae	*Plantago sparsiflora*	X	
Plantaginaceae	*Plantago virginica*	X	
Platanaceae	*Platanus occidentalis*	X	
Poaceae	*Agrostis stolonifera*	X	
Poaceae	*Arundinaria gigantea*	X	
Poaceae	*Axonopus furcatus*		X
Poaceae	*Cenchrus longispinus*	X	
Poaceae	*Chasmanthium laxum*	X	
Poaceae	*Chasmanthium sessiliflorum*	X	
Poaceae	*Cynodon dactylon*	X	
Poaceae	*Dichanthelium commutatum*	X	
Poaceae	*Dichanthelium strigosum var. leucoblepharis*	X	
Poaceae	*Distichlis spicata*	X	
Poaceae	*Eremochloa ophiuroides*		X
Poaceae	*Glyceria striata*	X	
Poaceae	*Oplismenus hirtellus*	X	X
Poaceae	*Paspalum laeve*	X	
Poaceae	*Paspalum notatum*		X
Poaceae	*Piptochaetium avenaceum*	X	
Poaceae	*Poa annua*	X	
Poaceae	*Sorghum halepense*	X	
Poaceae	*Spartina alterniflora*	X	
Poaceae	*Spartina bakeri*	X	
Poaceae	*Spartina cynosuroides*	X	
Poaceae	*Sphenopholis obtusata*	X	
Poaceae	*Sporobolus indicus*		X
Poaceae	*Stenotaphrum secundatum*	X	
Polemoniaceae	*Phlox carolina*	X	
Polygonaceae	*Polygonum hydropiperoides*	X	
Polygonaceae	*Polygonum persicaria*	X	
Polygonaceae	*Rumex acetosella*	X	
Polypodiaceae	*Polypodium polypodioides*	X	
Pontederiaceae	*Pontederia cordata*	X	
Primulaceae	*Samolus valerandi ssp. parviflorus*	X	
Pteridaceae	*Pteris etata*	X	
Rosaceae	*Agrimonia parviflora*	X	
Rosaceae	*Geum canadense*	X	
Rosaceae	*Potentilla simplex*	X	
Rosaceae	*Prunus angustifolia*	X	
Rosaceae	*Prunus caroliniana*	X	X
Rosaceae	*Prunus serotina*	X	X
Rosaceae	*Prunus umbellata*	X	
Rosaceae	*Pyrus communis*	X	
Rosaceae	*Rubus trivialis*	X	
Rubiaceae	*Cephalanthus occidentalis*	X	X
Rubiaceae	*Diodia teres*	X	
Rubiaceae	*Galium aparine*		X
Rubiaceae	*Galium hispidulum*	X	
Rubiaceae	*Galium lanceolatum*	X	
Rubiaceae	*Galium obtusum*	X	
Rubiaceae	*Galium pilosum*	X	

Table A-1. Continued.

Family	Species	NPSpecies	This Study
Rubiaceae	*Galium tinctorium*	X	
Rubiaceae	*Houstonia procumbens*	X	
Sapotaceae	*Sideroxylon reclinatum*		X
Sapotaceae	*Sideroxylon tenax*	X	
Scrophulariaceae	*Gratiola virginiana*	X	
Scrophulariaceae	*Nuttallanthus canadensis*	X	
Scrophulariaceae	*Paulownia tomentosa*	X	
Scrophulariaceae	*Verbascum thapsus*	X	
Scrophulariaceae	*Veronica arvensis*	X	
Smilacaceae	*Smilax auriculata*	X	
Smilacaceae	*Smilax bona-nox*	X	X
Smilacaceae	*Smilax glauca*	X	
Smilacaceae	*Smilax laurifolia*		X
Smilacaceae	*Smilax pumila*	X	
Smilacaceae	*Smilax smallii*	X	
Solanaceae	*Physalis viscosa*	X	
Solanaceae	*Solanum carolinense*	X	
Symplocaceae	*Symplocos tinctoria*	X	X
Theaceae	*Gordonia lasianthus*		X
Thelypteridaceae	*Thelypteris dentata*	X	
Ulmaceae	*Celtis laevigata*	X	X
Urticaceae	*Boehmeria cylindrica*	X	
Verbenaceae	*Callicarpa americana*	X	X
Verbenaceae	*Lantana camara*	X	
Verbenaceae	*Phyla nodiflora*	X	X
Violaceae	*Viola affinis*	X	
Violaceae	*Viola lanceolata*	X	
Violaceae	*Viola palmata*	X	
Vitaceae	*Ampelopsis arborea*	X	X
Vitaceae	*Parthenocissus quinquefolia*	X	X
Vitaceae	*Vitis aestivalis*	X	
Vitaceae	*Vitis rotundifolia*	X	X